The New York Public Library

Stephen A. Schwarzman Building   A Beaux-Arts Landmark

Ingrid Steffensen   ART SPACES

The New York Public Library in association with
Scala Publishers Ltd

A Site at the Heart of the City

New York City, the intersection of 42nd Street and Fifth Avenue: one of the busiest corners in perhaps the most energetic city in the world. There, on the southwest corner, The New York Public Library's flagship building stands as an oasis of quiet amid cacophony, true democracy amid ferocious competition, learning amid commercialism, and softly gleaming white marble amid a jungle of glass, concrete, and asphalt. A landmark of Beaux-Arts architecture—classical, imposing, yet inviting—the Library is one of the defining institutions of New York City.

The area bounded by 40th and 42nd streets on the south and north, and by Fifth and Sixth avenues on the east and west, shared by the Library and the greensward known as Bryant Park, has a rich history going back to the Revolutionary War. In 1776 the site was a battleground for George Washington's troops as they fled British forces. After the War of Independence, the city of New York grew so rapidly that by 1800 the state government saw the need to create a plan to guide the northward development of the island of Manhattan. In 1811 a commission led by New York Mayor DeWitt Clinton produced the now familiar grid of Manhattan in an 8-foot-long map, known as the Commissioner's Plan. The plan had the advantage of great simplicity but the disadvantage of monotony; there were few breaks and no parkland in its relentless march north to 155th

∧ Croton Reservoir, 1850.

≪ The Library at dusk, May 20, 1995, during the celebration of the centennial of the founding of The New York Public Library.

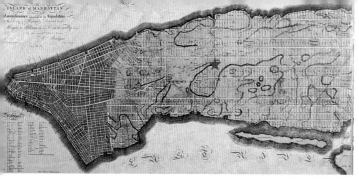

∧ A detail of the Commissioner's Plan of 1811; the star indicates the area that would become the site of Reservoir Square and, later, Bryant Park.

"Burning of the New York Crystal Palace, on Tuesday Oct. 5th. 1858," a lithograph by Currier & Ives.

Street. Central Park, the great "lungs" of the city, came into existence only after famed New York poet, editor, and parks advocate William Cullen Bryant called for such a space in 1844.

Bryant Park's origins lie in the construction in 1845 of the Distributing Reservoir of the Croton Aqueduct System, whose size necessitated another break in the short, numbered streets of the grid. The stark Egyptian Revival style—popular at the time, the style was also used at the old New York prison familiarly called "The Tombs"—was ameliorated by the designation of the empty space behind the reservoir as public land. Reservoir Square, as the space was known,

served as the site of America's first international industrial exposition, the New York Crystal Palace of 1853, modeled after the hugely successful Crystal Palace Exhibition in London in 1851. A large iron-and-glass greenhouse-style construction, the New York Crystal Palace saw, among other things, the first demonstration of the Otis elevators that would be so essential to the development of the city's skyscrapers. The Crystal Palace was destroyed by fire in 1858, leaving Reservoir Square empty once again. The square acquired its present name in 1884, when it was rededicated in honor of William Cullen Bryant, who had died in 1878.

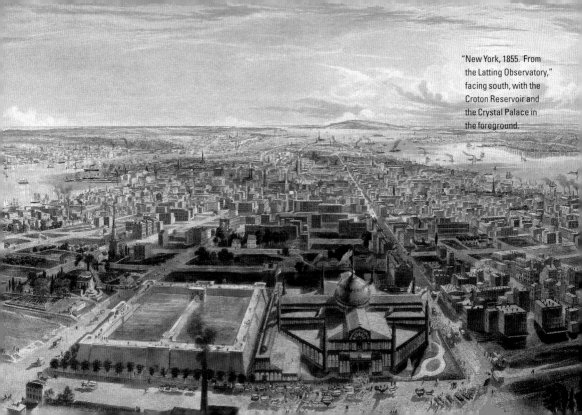

"New York, 1855. From the Latting Observatory," facing south, with the Croton Reservoir and the Crystal Palace in the foreground.

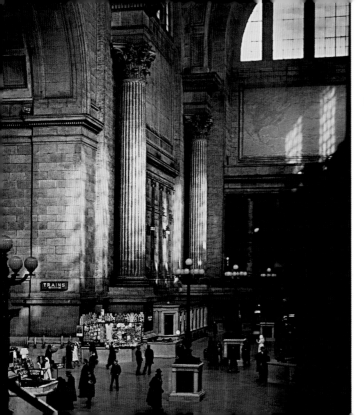

A Beaux-Arts Locus Evolves

In 1897, the Croton Reservoir site attracted the attention of the Trustees of the recently founded New York Public Library. The intersection of 42nd Street and Fifth Avenue was well situated to serve Library patrons from across the region and even the nation, located as it was between the transportation hubs represented by the existing Grand Central Depot at 42nd Street and Park Avenue, and the anticipated Pennsylvania Station, at 33rd Street and Seventh Avenue, planning for which had begun in 1895. A new Grand Central Terminal, with a magnificent Beaux-Arts façade by Warren & Wetmore, was completed in 1913. The fortunate visitor to the Library who today

< Carrère & Hastings's drawing (detail) of The New York Public Library's Fifth Avenue façade, showing the triple-arched central portico, ca. 1902.

Grand Central Terminal, completed in 1913, photographed in the 1920s.

≪ Interior of the old Pennsylvania Station, completed in 1910, photographed in 1939.

arrives in New York City via Grand Central and passes through its starry, vaulted (and recently restored) main concourse can experience the same spatial exhilaration envisioned a century ago. The original Pennsylvania Station, the most ambitious project to be undertaken by the firm of McKim, Mead & White up to that time, was commissioned by the President of the Long Island Railroad, Alexander J. Cassatt—brother of the American Impressionist painter Mary Cassatt—in 1902. Completed in 1910, Pennsylvania Station was the largest building ever constructed for rail travel, and its soaring waiting room, based on the great vaulted central hall of the Roman Baths of Caracalla, added a feeling of ancient grandeur to the experience of the modern traveler. These two train stations and The New York Public Library all had their genesis in the period often termed the American Renaissance (1876–1914), when railroad moguls and business tycoons, as well as cities and major public institutions, commissioned grand architectural symbols of their lofty cultural missions. From 1913 until 1963, when Pennsylvania Station was torn down, these three great buildings would serve as a Beaux-Arts locus of New York architecture.

> The earliest known photograph of the British Museum Library's great domed reading room, which opened in 1857.

South Hall of the Astor Library in New York City, from *Harper's Weekly*, October 2, 1875.

A Testament to Cultural Aspiration

A national trend toward building public libraries began with the 1888 design for the Boston Public Library. By 1930, almost every major city in the United States had constructed a large public library building. This era also saw the construction of many of the nation's most important state capitol buildings, museums, university campuses, and concert halls. The 1893 World's Columbian Exposition in Chicago had created a new ideal for these buildings, putting into architectural reality the budding vision that would become the City Beautiful movement, which embraced Beaux-Arts classicism, formal landscape settings, and a high cultural mission. The

New York Public Library would participate in all of these ideals.

Until 1895, New York City had relied on libraries formed and maintained by private individuals. Two of the most important were the Astor Library on Lafayette Street, founded in 1852 by John Jacob Astor, one of the richest men in America; and the Lenox Library, formed by another wealthy bibliophile, James Lenox, who built his library in 1870 on upper Fifth Avenue between 70th and 71st streets. Both libraries were privately run; neither was truly public in the modern sense.

Then, in 1886, Samuel J. Tilden, the former Governor of New York, left a portion of his substantial fortune for the founding of a free public library in New York City. The body charged with overseeing this legacy, the Tilden Trust, subsequently joined with these private libraries in a historic merger on May 23, 1895, forming a new entity, The New York Public Library, Astor, Lenox and Tilden Foundations, whose mission was to "establish and maintain a free public library and reading-room in the City of New York." The next year, Library President John Bigelow pushed a bill through the state legislature authorizing the razing of the Croton Reservoir and the construction of a new building on its site. The Library was thus poised to erect a monument worthy of its cultural aspirations.

∧ Among the American precursors to The New York Public Library were, left, McKim, Mead & White's Boston Public Library and, center and right, the World's Columbian Exposition of 1893, whose pavilions and halls embodied the Beaux-Arts ideals of the City Beautiful movement.

> In its sweeping, unified, horizontal façade, McKim, Mead & White's design is reminiscent of the firm's plan for the Boston Public Library.

The design by Brite & Bacon is dominated by an oversized dome that marks the main reading room.

>> George B. Post's design is typically austere and commanding, but wasn't even a finalist.

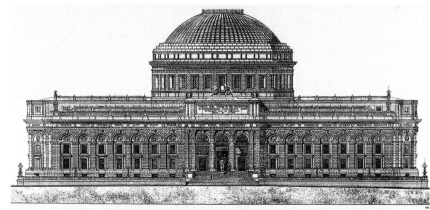

COMPETITIVE DESIGN FOR THE NEW YORK PUBLIC LIBRARY.
BRITE & BACON, ARCHITECTS.

A Fin-de-Siècle Architectural Event:
The 1897 Competition

The 1897 competition for the design of the new Library was a signal event in fin-de-siècle architectural circles, drawing illustrious contestants whose submissions reflected the project's ambitious ideals. The Library's Trustees decided to hold, first, an open competition for local, lesser-known architects; and, second, a closed, invitational one for established architects. The winners of the first phase would then be judged against the invitees of the second. The response to the first competition, which was open to all architects practicing in the greater New York City area, was tremendous, with eighty-eight plans received by the July 15, 1897, deadline.

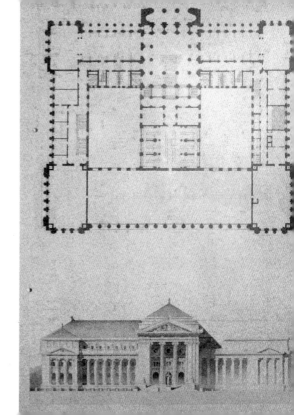

The contestants were guided by the Library's competition pamphlet, which specified the basic functions of the building and even provided a suggested floor plan. All of the competition designs that have survived were classical in style. The most illustrious future architect to participate in the preliminary contest was Henry Bacon of the firm of Brite & Bacon, who was later the architect of the Lincoln Memorial in Washington, D.C. His firm submitted an entry with a tremendous dome marking the main reading room on the second-story level, probably inspired by the great domed reading rooms of the British Library and the Bibliothèque nationale. In the second stage of the competition, one of the foremost architects of the day, George B. Post (designer of the New York Stock Exchange), submitted a commanding design; and the architects of the enormously influential Boston Public Library, McKim, Mead & White, also submitted an entry.

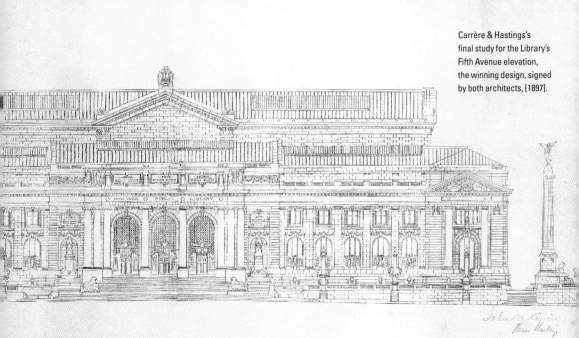

Carrère & Hastings's
final study for the Library's
Fifth Avenue elevation,
the winning design, signed
by both architects, [1897].

Architectural draftsmen in the
Carrère & Hastings workshop,
September 8, 1905.

Carrère and Hastings

John Merven Carrère

Thomas Hastings

Unexpectedly, the prize went to the youngest and least experienced of the invited architects, John Merven Carrère (1858–1911) and Thomas Hastings (1860–1929). So successful was their completed design that they were subsequently commissioned to design fourteen of the branch libraries funded by steel magnate Andrew Carnegie. Later, they would also design the building for Henry Clay Frick that now houses the Frick Collection. In accordance with their training at the École nationale supérieure des Beaux-Arts in Paris, their design is imposing and classical, yet eminently logical. The silhouette of the building allowed its interior spaces to be clearly "read": the central distribution space of the main hallways and staircases was marked by the mass of the entrance portico, and the great gabled form of the third-floor main reading room was lifted above the general mass of the structure. This feature, a controversial innovation first suggested by Library Director John Shaw Billings, was designed to elevate the seeker of knowledge both physically and metaphorically above everyday life as well as above the noise and dirt of the street. Together, the Library's Director and the architects created a building that was well-organized and functional, yet beautiful and inspiring.

The Beaux-Arts System of Design

In the nineteenth century, the École des Beaux-Arts (School of Fine Arts) in Paris, where Carrère and Hastings received their training, was the most renowned and respected architectural training ground in the world. With origins in the royal artistic aspirations of Louis XIV (1643–1715), the École drew aspiring architects from all over Europe. In 1846, Richard Morris Hunt, who would later design the Fifth Avenue façade of the Metropolitan Museum of Art in New York City, became the first American to enroll there.

Beaux-Arts classicism, as it is sometimes called, is an eclectic style combining ancient Greek and Roman models with ideas drawn from the Italian Renaissance and seventeenth-century France, and buildings in the style are often both colossal in size and richly ornamented. A typical Beaux-Arts plan was distinguished by interlocking geometric configurations, often disposed in hallways grouped around large central courtyards, such as may be found in the design for The New York Public Library. Great emphasis also attached to ceremonial progress through the building, as visitors encountered various paths—grand staircases, ceremonial forecourts, lengthy hallways—to its inner recesses, before arriving at the space at the heart of the building that answered to its principal function.

> Grand Escalier of Charles Garnier's Paris Opera (1861–74), the high point of École des Beaux-Arts architectural design.

≫ Detail of the Paris Opera's outer foyer, showing the eclectic, richly ornamented character of Beaux-Arts style.

A Monumental Undertaking

The immense project of building the Library began in 1899, and lasted twelve years. It took 500 workers two years to dismantle the massive Croton Reservoir. Construction costs came to $9,002,523—over $168 million in 2002 terms. Carrère & Hastings used 530,000 cubic feet of white Vermont marble to sheathe the exterior of the building and provide its interior detailing, making the Library the largest marble structure erected up to that time in the United States. The exterior marble has an average depth of 12 inches, behind which is a traditional load-bearing masonry wall, consisting of 4 feet of solid brick.

Every complicated classical detail, both exterior and interior, had to be hand-carved by masons and

< Inside the Fifth Avenue portico, July 2, 1906.

≪ Men hoisting marble during construction, September 28, 1906.

^ From left to right:

Hauling marble for the new Library building from a quarry in Dorset, Vermont, to the railroad, August 1904.

The Fifth Avenue entrance without its marble, July 3, 1906.

Artisans at work in the plaster carving workshop in the unfinished building, June 10, 1902.

carpenters trained in Old World techniques. Many of the craftsmen were French, German, and Italian immigrants, who supplied skills and talent brought with them from Europe. The architects custom-designed, and craftsmen executed, every fitting and fixture, and the finest artists of the day provided further embellishment by creating the building's sculptural and painted ornament. The artisans, contractors, and workmen collaborated so harmoniously with the architects that they achieved their goal with an unusually high degree of precision—for example, of a $3 million expenditure for the interior, only $600 was charged to errors.

Two months before the official opening of the new Library, tragedy struck when John Carrère was killed in an automobile accident. The Parks Commissioner directed that, on March 6, 1911, "for the first and only time before its completion, the doors of the Library [would] be opened to all the people," so that the body of the dedicated young architect could lie in state in Astor Hall.

The completed Library, photographed ca. 1916–22 by Wurts Brothers.

The New York Public Library's first president, John Bigelow (at center, striding with top hat and cane), arriving for opening day festivities, May 23, 1911.

Opening Day

The Library opened formally on May 23, 1911, to great fanfare, with President William Howard Taft present, as well as New York Governor John Alden Dix, New York City Mayor William Jay Gaynor, and crowds of people who embraced the Library from the start as one of the great monuments of the city. In his speech, President Taft elicited support for the new Library, putting it in a national context:

> The dedication of this beautiful structure for the spread of knowledge among the people marks not only the consummation of a noteworthy plan for bringing within

< Visitors queuing on opening day, *New-York Tribune*, May 24, 1911.

the grasp of the humblest and poorest citizen the opportunity for acquiring information on every subject of every kind, but it furnishes a model and example for other cities which have been struggling with the same problem, and points for them the true way.

In 1913, Mayor Gaynor said of the new Library, "Who can pass by that building for the first time without stopping? (I almost said kneeling down; but we don't kneel down as easily as that in New York City.)"

< The *Christian Herald* celebrated opening day with a cover showing the first visitors in Astor Hall.

The Façade:
A Great Artistic Collaboration

> The Arch of Constantine, a color etching from Pieter Schenk's *Roma aeterna* (1705).

Background: Carrère & Hastings's drawing of the two vases on the Fifth Avenue steps, undated.

The Library's architecture earned the building National Historic Landmark status in 1965. The central feature of the building's exterior is the great triple-arched portico, a visual metaphor of welcome and ingress, as well as a historical reference to antiquity. Its form is based upon the Roman triumphal arch, particularly on those of late antiquity possessing three arched openings, as, for example, the much-admired Arch of Constantine in Rome (312–315). Corinthian columns flank each arch, and the columns pair up to frame the central arch, emphasizing its importance as an entrance. This basic arrangement had been used previously by Richard Morris Hunt at the Metropolitan Museum of Art (designed 1895), and would be used again by Warren & Wetmore at Grand Central Terminal.

The exterior ornamentation of the building constitutes one of the great artistic collaborations of the turn of the last century, and a list of the artists who contributed to the embellishment of the terrace and Fifth Avenue (or east) façade of the Library reads like a "Who's Who" of American sculptors of the era. During the American Renaissance, there was a common ideal of collaboration among architects, sculptors, and painters—an ideal that hearkened back to the Italian Renaissance. It was believed that

> The Fifth Avenue façade and plaza from above, ca. 1936, highlighting the portico and the six attic figures.

such collaboration elevated all of the arts involved, and that the choice of important, historical, and ennobling subject matter was an indispensable component in the design of any major public monument. Therefore, both special artistry as well as symbolic resonance enhanced the figures adorning the building.

The utilitarian purpose of the flagpoles on the terrace, for example, does not lessen the artistic importance they serve in such a prominent spot, and they were thus carefully designed by architect Thomas Hastings. Thematically, they represent exploration and the spread of civilization around the world, for at their bases are seated four winged

figures, representing Navigation (symbolized by a boat), Discovery (a globe), Conquest (a sword), and Civilization (a book). Careful inspection will reveal cows' skulls, owls' heads, cornucopias, and turtles, making the rich surfaces teem with life. The bronze bases were cast in 1912 by the Tiffany Studios. Another important decorative element on the terraced approach to the Library is the great pair of vases flanking the stairs. These were inspired by engravings of ancient Roman vases by the eighteenth-century architect Giovanni Battista Piranesi, as well as by similar vases that ornament the terraces at the Palace at Versailles.

A personification—an abstract idea expressed in human form—was another way of both ennobling (through ideals) and enlivening (through use of the human figure) the surfaces and meanings of the building. And so, standing proudly above the Corinthian columns of the front portico are six colossal figures carved by Paul Wayland Bartlett (1865–1925), a sculptor who also worked on the New York Stock Exchange and the United States Capitol. The 11-foot-high allegorical figures represent some of the most important disciplines whose works are contained inside the building; depicted, from left to right, are History, Drama, Poetry, Religion, Romance, and Philosophy.

> Discovery, one of the four allegorical winged figures on the terrace flagpole pedestals.

Probably the most artistically notable exterior sculptures are the two fountains to either side of the portico. These were executed by Frederick MacMonnies (1863–1937), a sculptor who enriched New York with his work on the famous arch in Washington Square as well as the Nathan Hale statue in City Hall Park. To the right of the portico (the north side) is his fountain representing Truth as a hoary man seated on a sphinx (associated with timeless wisdom); the biblical inscription above his head reads, "Above all things, Truth beareth away the victory" (Apocrypha: 1 Esdras 3:12). To the left (or south side) of the portico is the idealized figure of Beauty. She sits on the back of the winged horse Pegasus,

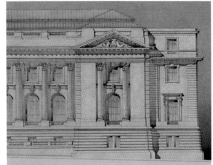

∧ Poetry (left) and Drama (right), two of the six attic sculptures by Paul Wayland Bartlett.

Carrère & Hastings's pencil and pen-and-ink drawing of the north wing of the Fifth Avenue façade, with the north pediment.

symbolizing inspiration and elevation above worldly concerns. Over her head is inscribed a passage from American poet John Greenleaf Whittier's "The Shadow and Light": "Beauty old yet ever new / eternal voice and inward word."

Finally, the important sculptor George Grey Barnard (1863–1917) contributed the sculpture in the two pediments crowning the corner pavilions at the south and north ends of the building. Pedimental sculpture is among the most difficult to execute, because the shallow triangle formed by the classical pediment ill accommodates the human figure. Furthermore, the pediments at the Library are relatively small. Barnard solved the

problem by filling the spaces with reclining figures, posed in heraldic, symmetrical fashion to either side of symbolic devices. The Arts (south pediment) are represented by a man with a hammer and chisel (doubtless celebrating the sculptor's own profession) and a woman with two large books, to either side of a globe, representing art's universality. In the north pediment, dedicated to History, an armored man rests his elbow on a book upon which a female figure inscribes the word "LIFE."

The jewel-like setting of the Library, standing apart from the city grid and harbored within a park and a series of encircling terraces, allows

for a rare axial vista down East 41st Street culminating in a view of the great triple-arched portico of the main façade. The setting, the architecture, and the sculpture and decorative ornamentation of the Library's exterior thus all conspire to create a building whose exterior may itself be read as a synopsis of the accomplishments of poets, writers, scholars, artists, and indeed of humanism itself—a noble repository for the intellectual riches that are housed within.

< The south fountain with the statue of Beauty by Frederick MacMonnies, photographed by Wurts Brothers.

The Library Lions

Of all the exquisitely executed sculpture that attracts the eye as one approaches the Library, none has so captured the public imagination as the pair of guardian lions flanking the steps leading to the main entrance on Fifth Avenue. Modeled in pink Tennessee marble by noted animal sculptor Edward Clark Potter (1857–1923), they were carved by the Piccirilli Brothers, the finest stone carvers of the time.

As mascots of the Library, the lions have been adorned for special occasions over the years—the dignified creatures have tolerantly endured everything from evergreen wreaths during the holiday season to hard hats during periods of construction, to Yankees and Mets caps during baseball season,

reminders of the affectionate regard in which they are held by all. During their long residency, the Library lions have acquired various nicknames, including "Leo Astor and Leo Lenox," "Lord Astor and Lady Lenox," and, perhaps most famously, "Patience and Fortitude" (so dubbed by New York Mayor Fiorello LaGuardia for the qualities he felt New Yorkers would need to endure the hardships of the Great Depression). Having appeared by now in countless cartoons, prints, photographs, movies, and television programs, Patience and Fortitude have become beloved icons, instantly recognizable as representatives of The New York Public Library as a whole.

^ Cover of the May 22, 1995, issue of *The New Yorker* by Edward Sorel, celebrating the Centennial of The New York Public Library.

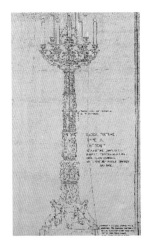

∧ An Astor Hall *torchère*,
depicted in an early lantern
slide and in Carrère &
Hastings's 1909 drawing.

The Interior:
A Regal Procession of Spaces

For the interior spaces of the Library, Carrère &
Hastings also followed the Beaux-Arts approach
to planning. With the decision to place the main
reading room on the third floor, their thinking was
guided by the idea that the architectural progres-
sion of the spaces of the building should follow a
logical, hierarchical sequence from the most easily accessible and public spaces, to the most
removed, scholarly retreats. Changes in the loca-
tions of divisions over the years have modified that
original idea to a degree, but it is interesting to
know something of it as one explores the building.

> Astor Hall, photographed from the second-floor gallery, looking east.

THE FIRST FLOOR

Astor Hall

Today, most visitors begin a tour of the Library by proceeding through a series of ever more enclosed spaces: from the exterior steps, past the lions, through the sheltering portico, and into the gracious space of Astor Hall. One of the most magnificent interiors in New York, Astor Hall achieves its magnificence less through sheer size—many New York spaces are larger than its 76 by 47 feet—than through its proportions and attention to detail. The scale is grand, to be sure, but never overwhelming. The use of vaulting—a self-supporting roof based on the structural principle of the arch—

Astor Hall, an early panoramic view.

> Astor Hall, photographed from one of the two great staircases leading from the hall to the second floor of the Library.

is technically ambitious and in itself a reference to the great vaulted spaces of Roman antiquity. Although the shallow, segmental-arched vaulting rises 37 feet overhead, the space is brought back to the human scale through such elements as the four marble *torchères* standing sentry at the edges of the room, and by the stairs that rise at either side of the great hall and seem to float away without supports beyond the first turning, on their way to the second floor. The architects achieved unity and sumptuousness through the exclusive use of white marble, which covers every available surface; especially remarkable is the self-supporting marble cladding of the vaults. The marble of Astor Hall is from Vermont; that of the hallway beyond is the famous Pentelic marble from Greece, which was also used for the Parthenon in Athens.

Exhibition Spaces

Past the second set of *torchères*, through an arched entrance way, and beyond a sumptuously decorated pair of cast bronze doors, the visitor enters the D. Samuel and Jeane H. Gottesman Exhibition Hall, larger (at 83 by 77 feet) even than Astor Hall, and the most elaborate public interior space on the first floor. Vermont marble piers fronted by a total of 24 monolithic, Ionic columns support one of the most intricately carved ceilings in the country, executed by the craftsman Maurice Grieve. The visitor who

takes the time to look up will find carved into the coffers of the oak ceiling angels, cherubs, satyr masks, fruited garlands, and a great deal of foliate ornament. Adapted to administrative use during World War II, Gottesman Hall was completely restored in 1984. Today, most visitors to the space come to see one of the many changing exhibitions that highlight the Library's vast and distinguished collections.

Another, smaller space on the first floor, recently renovated and restored to its original function, is the handsome Sue and Edgar Wachenheim III Gallery. Designated as a small exhibition hall when the building first opened, it was converted during the lean years of World War II to a book canteen for servicemen, and was subsequently transformed into the Frederick Lewis Allen Room, reserved for writers with book contracts. Both Gottesman Hall and the Wachenheim Gallery have now come full circle in their historical function within the building.

The DeWitt Wallace Periodical Room and Its Murals

The long transverse gallery between Astor Hall and Gottesman Hall connects the most public axis of the first floor with the spaces that run around the building's periphery, today housing, clockwise from the north end, the Irma and Paul

< The renovated D. Samuel
and Jeane H. Gottesman
Exhibition Hall, 1985.

> The south-north corridor
on the first floor.

Milstein Division of United States History, Local History and Genealogy, the Map Division, the Library Shop, the DeWitt Wallace Periodical Room, and the Microforms Reading Room.

In the Periodical Room, a visitor may ask for a magazine or journal, and read it at leisure, appropriately surrounded by mural paintings depicting New York buildings associated with the publishing industry. The murals were part of a major restoration effort completed in 1983, through a bequest from DeWitt Wallace, founder of *Reader's Digest* magazine. Wallace had in fact spent the formative years of the *Digest* in the Periodical Room, condensing articles for what would become the world's most widely read magazine.

< A view of the DeWitt Wallace
Periodical Room, showing
(unobstructed) two of the
Richard Haas murals, from
left: the Reader's Digest
Building (over doorway) and
City Hall and Newspaper Row.

Contemporary New York artist Richard Haas (born 1936) executed the reading room's murals based on photographs of thirteen magazine and newspaper headquarters buildings, including, from the left, as you enter the room: Charles Scribner's Sons; the McGraw-Hill Building; the Hearst Building; Reader's Digest Building; the Look Building; City Hall and Newspaper Row; Park Row, Old Post Office; the Puck Building; Harper and Brothers; the Evening Post; Herald Square; Times Square; and the Time-Life Building. The super-realistic approach employed by Haas makes each mural appear almost like a *trompe l'oeil*, or "fool the eye," window puncturing the wall, rather than a painting simply hanging upon it.

^ Haas murals of, from left:
the 25-story Times building
and the Time-Life Building.

^ Haas murals of, from left:
Charles Scribner's Sons,
the McGraw-Hill Building,
and the Hearst Building.

< The old circulating library in the room with the glass and cast-iron dome on the ground floor, ca. 1911.

THE GROUND FLOOR
A Glass and Cast-Iron Dome
Below the first floor—that is, on the ground floor—is the spectacular Celeste Bartos Forum, fully refurbished and rededicated in 1986. Originally the Central Circulation Room of the Library (an early form of The Branch Libraries), this marble-paneled room, dominated by a glorious, 30-foot-high glass and cast-iron (or "ferrovitreous") dome, recalls the Crystal Palace that once stood nearly on the same spot. Inspired by Henri Labrouste's main reading room for the Bibliothèque nationale in Paris, the Bartos Forum now serves as an elegant setting for public

lectures, concerts, and films, and can accommo-
date up to 500 people. Interestingly, the relegation
of such industrial materials as cast iron to the lower
level of the Library was symptomatic of the lesser
status accorded the products of engineering during the American Renaissance period. The ground
floor is also home to the Dorot Jewish Division, one
of the world's great collections of Judaica, which
was renovated and renamed in honor of the Dorot
Foundation in 1986.

< The room—now
  the Celeste Bartos
  Forum—today.

∧ The Soichi Noma Reading Room of the Asian and Middle Eastern Division.

A view toward East 41st Street through one of the arches in the second-floor gallery, showing part of an exhibition on the Library's history in the Jill Kupin Rose Gallery.

THE SECOND FLOOR

Scholarly Enclaves and the Trustees' Retreat

Proceeding upward brings a visitor to the second-floor gallery, where distinctive arches provide a view of Astor Hall from above and, beyond it, Fifth Avenue. Off a central transverse corridor are two of the specialized language divisions of the Library: the Slavic and Baltic and the Asian and Middle Eastern divisions. Also on the second floor are rooms set aside for scholars: the Wertheim Study, for researchers involved in long-term projects; the Frederick Lewis Allen Room, for writers with signed book contracts; and the Dorothy and Lewis B. Cullman Center for Scholars and Writers, home to a fellowship program.

One of the interesting behind-the-scenes rooms on the second floor, to be visited only with special permission, is the Trustees Room. Befitting its purpose as a more intimate space for management meetings and formal gatherings, the Trustees Room is paneled in rich, dark walnut, and hung with seventeenth-century Flemish tapestries. Of special note is the fireplace, upon which may be found two high-relief carved maidens, a pair of snakes, and masks of Minerva, ancient goddess of wisdom, and Hercules, the ancient hero renowned for his strength. Between

> The elaborately carved marble chimneybreast and fireplace in the Trustees Room.

THE CITY OF NEW YORK HAS ERECTED THIS
BUILDING FOR THE FREE USE OF ALL THE PEOPLE

MCMX

I LOOK TO THE DIFFUSION OF LIGHT AND EDUCATION
AS THE RESOURCE MOST TO BE RELIED ON FOR
AMELIORATING THE CONDITION PROMOTING THE VIRTUE
AND ADVANCING THE HAPPINESS OF MAN.

the two maidens is inscribed a quotation from Thomas Jefferson that may well serve to express the mission of the Library as a whole: "I look to the diffusion of light and education as the resource most to be relied on for ameliorating the condition promoting the virtue and advancing the happiness of man."

< Clockwise, from upper left:

The bottom panel of the bronze grille-gate at the south end of the first-floor corridor.

The catfish and cattails on the keystone of the drinking fountain of the second-floor gallery.

A bronze lion mask, a detail of the gallery's drinking fountain.

Bucrane and ox hooves ornament the base of a *torchère* in Astor Hall.

A Feast of Decorative Detail

he architects lavished no less attention on the interior of the Library than they did on the exterior. Every detail was drawn to scale and executed to custom specifications. From overall conception to the smallest finishing—down to door handles, water fountains, and wastebaskets!—every surface and every object was unique to the building. The rich classical detailing enlivens stone, wood, metal, and stucco with motifs from mythology, the animal world, and the natural world. A careful observer will spot satyrs, griffins, sphinxes, nymphs, and cherubs, all taken from the pantheon of classical myth. Lurking in the decoration is a veritable zoo, as well; one may find cow skulls (called "bucrania"), bears, birds, fish, dolphins, and the ever-present lions, a leitmotif repeated from the famous exterior sculptures and carried throughout the building's interior. Surrounding these more recognizable forms are natural and abstract motifs from antiquity: fruit garlands, foliate ornamentation (intertwining "guilloches" and spiraling "rinceaux"), and framed heraldic emblems (oval "cartouches"), to name a few. Note, as well, the New York City coat of arms adorning the table pedestals in the Wallace Periodical Room and the Rose Main Reading Room.

Background: Carrère & Hastings's drawing of the bronze railing at the third-floor landing, the design incorporating swans evolving into acanthus leaves, 1909.

< The Rotunda ceiling, decorated with Edward Laning's painting of Prometheus bringing the gift of fire—symbolic of inspiration and knowledge—to man.

» The McGraw Rotunda and two of the four murals of Edward Laning's cycle, *Story of the Recorded Word*—"Gutenberg Showing a Proof to the Elector of Mainz" (left) and "The Linotype—Mergenthaler and Whitelaw Reid" (right); above the doorway is Laning's lunette painting, "The Student."

THE THIRD FLOOR

The McGraw Rotunda

Further ascent brings the visitor to one of the most magnificent progressions of interior spaces to be found in New York City—or, for that matter, anywhere. If, as the architects intended, one has climbed the stairs, arrival at the McGraw Rotunda provides a sense of spatial expansion as it soars over one's head, and the ceiling showing Prometheus in the clouds even suggests the reaching of a mountain's summit. The term "rotunda" generally refers to a circular structure, usually covered by a dome, but here it is a rectangular space covered by a barrel vault, like Astor Hall below it, but with a higher, fully semicircular, profile. Richly carved and gilt wood here replaces the marble of Astor Hall, and the space is further enriched by a mural painting cycle—a series of related paintings, often telling a story—depicting the *Story of the Recorded Word*.

Story of the Recorded Word, a Mural Cycle by Edward Laning

This cycle was painted from 1938 to 1942 by Illinois native Edward Laning (1906–1981), under the auspices of the Federal Art Project (FAP) of the Works Progress Administration (WPA), the Depression-era government program estab-

Edna Barnes Salomon Room
116

> The Edna Barnes
  Salomon Room, with
  a glimpse through the
  doorway to the McGraw
  Rotunda and the Laning
  mural "Moses with the
  Tablets of the Law."

lished in 1935 under President Franklin Delano Roosevelt. One of many WPA projects, the FAP employed thousands of un- or underemployed artists to paint murals in schools, hospitals, and post offices throughout the country.

Laning's panels, executed in a realistic, neo-Renaissance style popular for FAP projects, mesh impressively with the original intention of the architects in their depiction of a relevant and ennobling subject, both inspiring and historically grounded. The chronological cycle begins with Moses bringing the word of God down from Mount Sinai, in the form of the Ten Commandments. The next mural depicts a medieval monk copying man-uscripts. Next, Johann Gutenberg is represented with his Bible—of which the Library possesses the first complete copy to reach American soil. America's contribution to the recorded word is embodied in a mural of Ottmar Mergenthaler, the inventor of the Linotype machine, who is shown with his invention and with Whitelaw Reid of *The New York Tribune*, the latter reading one of the newspapers that was the product of their collabo-ration. Presiding over all is the ceiling depicting Prometheus, divine thief and friend of humanity, bringing the gift of fire—symbolic of inspiration and knowledge—to man.

< The Prints and Photographs Study Room, the Miriam and Ira D. Wallach Division of Art, Prints and Photographs.

The reading room of the Carl H. Pforzheimer Collection of Shelley and His Circle, restored in 1993 by Peter Marino and Associates, is furnished with antiques from the original collector's home.

Special Collections Reading Rooms and Exhibition Spaces

From the McGraw Rotunda visitors may find their way to the various special collections and exhibition rooms grouped on the third floor: the Edna Barnes Salomon Room, an exhibition space; the reading room for the Print and Photography collections of the Miriam and Ira D. Wallach Division of Art, Prints and Photographs; the Henry W. and Albert A. Berg Collection of English and American Literature; and the Carl H. Pforzheimer Collection of Shelley and His Circle. Of special note are the paintings that line the walls of the Salomon Room, which include "The Blind Milton Dictating *Paradise Lost* to His Daughters," by Mikhaly Munkacsy. The third-floor corridors are also frequently used for exhibitions.

< The doorway to the Bill Blass
  Public Catalog Room, Room
  315, with Edward Laning's
  lunette painting, "Learning
  to Read."

The Heart of the Library:
The Bill Blass Public Catalog Room

The ultimate destination for most visitors, however, is the Bill Blass Public Catalog Room and, beyond it, the magnificent Rose Main Reading Room. Entering from the McGraw Rotunda, the visitor first encounters the Library's printed and computerized catalogs and the Information Desk, staffed by librarians of the General Research Division. The original building offered card catalogs (retired from use in 1983), in wooden drawers and cabinets, as the means to access the Library's holdings. Today, older materials are located through the 800 bound volumes that

> The Bill Blass Public
  Catalog Room in 2002.

The Public Catalog
Room in 1911.

reproduce the original catalog cards, and all
material acquired since 1971 is listed in The
Research Libraries' online catalog, CATNYP
(catnyp.nypl.org). Many pre-1971 cataloging
records have by now been retrospectively added
to CATNYP, as well.

The Library Stacks

> The Library's stacks, 2002.

Cross-sectional view of the stacks, from the cover of *Scientific American*, May 27, 1911. Instead of traditional load-bearing masonry, the stacks employed the stronger, lighter-weight materials of cast iron and steel to support the enormous weight of books housed within the original 88 miles of shelving, a technological innovation that received much attention in the press.

To request a book or periodical, the researcher fills out a call slip, takes it to the clerk at the desk, and receives a delivery number. The slip is then delivered to the stacks through a pneumatic tube system, which was part of the original building and is still, remarkably, in use.

Invisible to the visitor or researcher is the activity that is then set in motion, once an order is submitted. Below the Rose Main Reading Room are the original seven levels of stacks, which are closed to the public and which were designed to hold about 3.5 million volumes. The Library's stack space was expanded in 1992, below the ground level of Bryant Park, doubling the shelf capacity of the building to a generous 7 million volumes. Once a book is located amid the 125 miles of shelving, it is deposited onto a miniature elevator designed solely for transporting books, and then sent up to be collected in the Rose Main Reading Room. None of the books in this building can be borrowed; all must be used onsite.

The renovated
Deborah, Jonathan F. P.,
Samuel Priest, and
Adam Raphael Rose Main
Reading Room, 1998.

> Entry vestibule to the
Rose Main Reading Room.

Background: Carrère &
Hastings's drawing of the
doorway leading from the
Public Catalog Room to the
Main Reading Room, 1909.

The Rose Main Reading Room

To claim a requested item, the researcher must pass from the Bill Blass Public Catalog Room to the Rose Main Reading Room, through the monumental carved wooden entrance, above which are inscribed John Milton's moving words: "A good Booke is the pretious life-blood of a master-spirit, embalm'd and treasur'd up on purpose to a life beyond life." One of the largest uninterrupted interior spaces to be found in New York City, the Rose Main Reading Room measures 297 feet long (nearly two city blocks and about as long as a football field), 78 feet wide, and 51 feet high. It provides seating for 636 readers at custom-carved desks, under magnificent chandeliers and an extraordinary ceiling, all newly restored. Until recently, years of unfortunate neglect had diminished the effect of the room: blackout paint from World War II still obscured the beautiful high windows. Over time, too, half of the 23,000-square-foot space had been encroached upon by offices, as well as by the Library's photocopy and microforms service center. Library Trustee Sandra Priest Rose and her husband, Frederick P. Rose, funded the restoration effort in honor of their four children—Deborah, Jonathan F. P., Samuel Priest, and Adam Raphael Rose—for whom the room was named on its dedication in

< The Main Reading Room
under construction,
June 24, 1907.

A gilt winged cherub on
the ceiling of the Rose
Main Reading Room.

1998. The restoration effort also discreetly modernized and expanded the information technologies available in the room—there are now, for example, power outlets and data ports for laptop computers at many seats.

Carrère and Hastings gave careful thought to the organization of such a large space, which they subdivided into more manageable portions at floor level. A large wooden pavilion in the center of the room houses the delivery staff and mechanisms and divides the space into the North and South Halls. Here, readers wait for their books on the bench in front of the indicator board in the South Hall; when the assigned number lights up, the book may be claimed and taken to a table. Encircling the rows of desks, a 20,000-book open-shelf reference collection resides on shelving on two levels.

At each end of the Main Reading Room may be found the entrances to specialized departments: the Brooke Russell Astor Reading Room for Rare Books and Manuscripts, entered through the North Hall, and the Art and Architecture Collection, entered through the South Hall. Uniting all these disparate elements, the great expanse of ceiling soars unbroken overhead. Its decoration consists of recessed panels, called coffers, each intricately ornamented with twining and foliate motifs, and enriched with cherubs, angels, satyr masks, fruit,

and other classical motifs. These combine to surround three luminous paintings on canvas of sky and clouds by artist Yohannes Aynalem inspired by the Old Masters and later emulators, including Tintoretto and J.M.W. Turner; these new paintings replaced the original murals, which had deteriorated badly over the years.

The New South Court Building

The illusion of generous spaciousness endowed by the Library's setting adjacent to Bryant Park conceals an ever-growing need for additional space. Various solutions have been found for this problem, from creating new research libraries in altogether separate buildings, to burrowing underground for additional stack space. The integrity of the building—not to mention the landmark status that both the Library and the park enjoy—forbids any exterior changes or additions.

One of the last possible frontiers for such buildings is inward expansion; namely, reconfiguring previously unused or underused interior spaces. The largest unclaimed interior space remaining

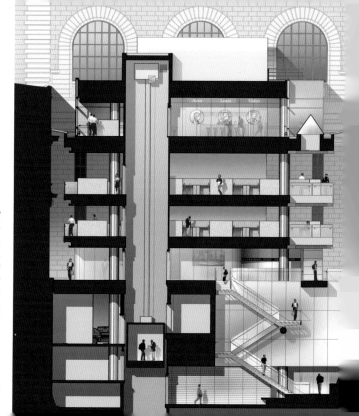

< Looking up toward the
skylight from the atrium
at the main entrance of
South Court.

≪ A corner of the modern
new South Court,
constructed within
the walls of the original
1911 building.

within the Library's walls at the turn of the twenty-first century was the open south courtyard, a vacuum in the dense fabric of the Library building. Invisible from the exterior, in 2002 the south courtyard was filled in by the architectural firm Davis Brody Bond with the first important above-ground addition to the building since its completion in 1911. The new South Court is a six-story freestanding building-within-a-building complex, a transparent glass envelope cantilevered out to within 4 feet of the marble walls to reveal the interior courtyard while enclosing spaces dedicated to the new information age technology. Entered from Astor Hall, the public portion of the complex is the Celeste Bartos Education Center, including a 24-seat Visitors' Theater, two classrooms, and a 178-seat auditorium with multimedia and webcasting capabilities. Much-needed administrative offices, a loading dock, and some parking facilities occupy the remaining space.

An aerial view of Bryant Park with The New York Public Library at left. From this perspective, the rear of the building serves as a backdrop to the formally designed park. Below the arched windows that light the Rose Main Reading Room, the alternating vertical stripes of stone and glass hint at the seven levels of book stacks within. A complete restoration of Bryant Park was completed in 1992, and two restaurants, designed by Hardy Holzman Pfeiffer LLP to blend delicately with the landscape, now complement the rear façade of the Library.

IF CARRÈRE & HASTINGS'S masterpiece and The New York Public Library have become inseparable in the public eye, it is because of the building's genius, its timeless elegance. Today, at the center of one of the great modern cities of the world, it remains a potent, even indispensable, symbol of the permanent ideals of intellectual exploration and freedom of thought. Despite—or perhaps because of—its nineteenth-century Beaux-Arts design, The New York Public Library, though sanctioned by the past, is triumphant as a twenty-first-century enterprise.

We would like to acknowledge with thanks the contributions of Jeanne Bornstein, staff curator of the exhibition *Building The New York Public Library* (December 1989–August 1997); Margaret Kable, Head Docent; and James Moske, Archivist, The New York Public Library Archives. Special thanks also to Erica Stoller and Susan Herpel of Esto Photographics, Inc.

ILLUSTRATION CREDITS

© Peter Aaron/Esto: front cover (right), 2, 27, 28 (left), 33, 36, 38, 44 (left & right), 48, 49, 50, 51 (left & right), 52, 53 (above), 54 (above), 55, 56 (right), 58, 59, 61, back cover; Maria Alos: 46; Courtesy of Avery Architectural and Fine Arts Library, Columbia University in the City of New York: 10 (below), from *The American Architect and Building News* 58, no. 1136 (October 2, 1897), plate [5]; Courtesy of the Boston Public Library, Print Department: 9 (left); Whitney Cox, courtesy of M (Group), New York: 45; Courtesy of Davis Brody Bond, LLP Architects and Planners: 60; © Anne Day: 30; Don Hamerman: 43; © Elliott Kaufman, courtesy of Hardy Holzman Pfeiffer Associates LLP: 62; © Peter Mauss/Esto: 40, 41 (left & right); Scott McKiernan: 39; Courtesy of the Museum of the City of New York, The McKim, Mead and White Collection: 10 (above); Collection of the New-York Historical Society: 11; Copyright © 1995 *The New Yorker* / Condé Nast Publications Inc. Reprinted by permission. All Rights Reserved: 31 (right); Don Pollard: front cover (left), 31 (left); James Rudnick: 57 (right).

NYPL Collections – Billy Rose Theatre Collection: 16, 17; Map Division: 4 (left); Milstein Division: 6, 22, 25, 31 (center); NYPL Archives: 7 (left), 12–13, 14, 18, 20 (left & right), 23 (above & below), 24 (left), 26 (above), 28 (right), 32 (left & right), 47, 56 (left), 57 (left); Science, Industry & Business Library: 54 (below); Wallach Division: 3, 4 (right), 5, 7 (right), 9 (center & right), 15 (above & below), 19, 20 (center), 21, 24 (right), 26 (below), 29, 34–35, 42, 53 (below).

ISBN: 978-1-85759-137-8

Printed and bound in China
10 9 8 7 6

Published by Scala Publishers Ltd in association with
The New York Public Library, Astor, Lenox and Tilden Foundations